D0643934

# THE INDIANAPOLIS 500

# THE INDIANAPOLIS 500

ROBERT K. KRISHEF

Lerner Publications Company ▪ Minneapolis, Minnesota

ACKNOWLEDGMENTS: The illustrations are reproduced through the courtesy of: pp. 4, 6, 9 (left, middle and right), 11, 12, 14, 15, 16, 19, 22 (top and bottom), 23 (top and bottom), 24, 27, 29 (top and bottom), 31, 35, 36, 38, 41, 44, 48, Indianapolis Motor Speedway; p. 7, The Goodyear Tire and Rubber Company; pp. 17, 18, 20, 32, 42, 45, 46, 47, 50 (bottom), United Press International; p. 25, Vernon J. Biever; p. 26, The Firestone Tire Company; p. 39, Wide World Photos; p. 50 (top), Ford News Department.

LIBRARY OF CONGRESS CATALOGING IN PUBLICATION DATA

**Krishef, Robert K.**
The Indianapolis 500.

(The Racing Books)
SUMMARY: A survey of the Indy 500 race, including information about the speedway, the race itself, the rules, the drivers, and a description of a typical race and its aftermath.

1. Indianapolis Speedway Race—Juvenile literature. [1. Indianapolis Speedway Race. 2. Automobile racing] I. Title.

GV1033.5.I55K74    796.7′2′0977252    73-22512
ISBN 0-8225-0412-X

Published simultaneously in Canada by J. M. Dent & Sons Ltd., Don Mills, Ontario.

Manufactured in the United States of America.

International Standard Book Number: 0-8225-0412-X
Library of Congress Catalog Card Number: 73-22512

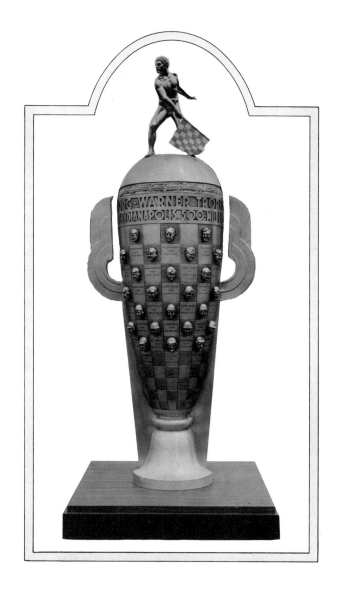

# FIRST IMPRESSIONS

Sponsors of the Indianapolis 500-mile race declare that it is "the greatest race in the world." Of course, because sponsors are so closely associated with the event, they are naturally enthusiastic about it. But even casual observers agree that the "Indy 500" is one of the world's most famous races.

When people call something "great" or "famous," they are placing high value on it. Their reason for doing this depends upon their point of view. And when it comes to evaluating the Indianapolis 500, there are as many points of view as there are groups interested in the race.

Naturally, Indy is a special challenge to the people who are most actively involved in the race—the drivers. Outstanding professional drivers want to compete against their equals. And because the Indianapolis Motor Speedway stands for excellence in racing, the country's best drivers eventually try to race there. It is sometimes said that professional drivers would compete at Indianapolis for the prestige alone. Perhaps so, but the cash prizes encourage them too. The Indianapolis 500 awards more prize money—over $1 million—than any other American automobile race. This amount is almost as much as that awarded by the other races of the United States Auto Club (USAC) championship circuit combined. Yet the Indy 500 is only 1 of 12 or more races on that circuit.

Of all the people who think the Indy 500 is "the greatest," no one feels more strongly about it than Anton (Tony) Hulman. Hulman owns the Indianapolis Motor Speedway, where the 500-mile race is held every Memorial Day weekend. For Hulman, each year's race represents the fulfillment of a commitment that he made in 1945. In that year,

The Indianapolis Motor Speedway

Hulman bought the then-deteriorated Speedway and determined to bring new life to it. The Speedway has been more successful under his direction than during any other period in its history.

For some people, the fame of the Indy 500 brings benefits. To Indianapolis community leaders, the 500 means more publicity than they could get in other ways. To the automobile industry and manufacturers of automobile parts, the 500 offers an opportunity to improve, test, and give publicity to their products.

For other people, however, the fame of the 500 brings problems. Newspaper and magazine reporters worry about getting stories. Policemen worry about handling traffic. And officials of the Speedway and of USAC, which supervises the race, worry about establishing safety measures. There is more reason to worry about safety measures now than ever before, for today's race cars travel twice as fast as those for which the Indianapolis Motor Speedway was originally designed.

The families of the drivers have a similar attitude toward the Indy 500. The race arouses fear in them because everybody knows that racing at Indy is dangerous. Risks are lessened when the drivers are skilled, but skill alone cannot eliminate the danger. As the prize money grows and the cars go faster, the competition becomes more and more hectic and thus more dangerous.

For the racing public, the Indianapolis 500 is something special. Each year, well over 500,000 people are on hand for the qualifying time-trials held during the two weekends preceding the race. At the actual race there are over 300,000 people in attendance. Many of these spectators follow racing faithfully and know a lot about it. Others do not know much about racing, and some do not even care. Yet, thousands of fans come to Indianapolis every Memorial Day weekend for the famous 500-mile championship-car race. For the fans in the stands and the many millions who follow the event on radio and television and who read about it in newspapers and magazines, the Indy 500 has become as much of an American tradition as the World Series.

How did the tradition begin? First, there was an idea. The man responsible for that idea was Carl G. Fisher, and the story of the Indy 500 starts with him.

**Mark Donohue races to victory in the 1972 Indy 500.**

# THE OWNERS

The Indianapolis Motor Speedway was opened in 1909 by Carl Fisher and three associates, Arthur Newby, Frank Wheeler, and James Allison. Since then, it has changed hands only twice. Edward (Eddie) Rickenbacker bought it in 1927, and Tony Hulman, the present owner, acquired it from Rickenbacker in 1945.

Fisher, Rickenbacker, and Hulman were all blessed with salesmanship, good business sense, and determination. They were sports-minded, too, and they learned to compete vigorously in whatever they did, regardless of any obstacles facing them. Hulman, for example, was an all-around athlete in his youth. He set pole-vaulting records in high school, starred in football at Yale University, and ran the high hurdles for Yale in international track meets. In 1923, he won the international high hurdles championship at Wembley, England.

Rickenbacker was also a sportsman. A racing enthusiast, he drove in the Indianapolis 500 five times. Then, when World War I broke out, Rickenbacker became an airplane pilot and a war hero, shooting down 26 enemy planes. As a civilian during World War II, Rickenbacker undertook a special government mission. He was enroute to a secret meeting with General Douglas MacArthur when his plane crash-landed in the Pacific Ocean. Rickenbacker and six others survived 24 days at sea in life rafts before being rescued.

Carl Fisher was one of the daredevils of his day. He raced in, with, or on practically anything that moved—bicycles, motorboats, balloons, and the newest form of transportation, the "horseless carriage."

The invention of the automobile had created a new sport, for proud car owners naturally wanted to see whose car could go faster. In the late 1890s and early 1900s, however, not everyone realized just how much the automobile would change passen-

Carl Fisher

Left to right: Henry Ford, Arthur Newby, Frank Wheeler, Carl Fisher, and James Allison

Eddie Rickenbacker

ger travel. But Carl Fisher did. Soon he was selling cars in Indianapolis as well as racing them. At that time, Indianapolis was the center of automotive manufacturing—the "Detroit" of its day.

From his experience as both an automobile salesman and a race-car driver, Fisher had become aware of two problems. First, he was not satisfied with the quality of cars being built in the United States. He believed that the industry needed a "proving ground" where the endurance and performance of automobiles could be tested and improved. No such facility was available, however. Nor

was there any facility to take advantage of the tremendous popularity that auto racing was expected to have. This was the second problem.

When Fisher had raced in Europe, he had been impressed with the quality of the drivers and the cars. This quality was due, he felt, to the high standards of performance demanded in European road racing. But this form of racing was not possible in America because here there were no roads long enough or smooth enough for road races. The only race courses in America at that time were small, dirt tracks.

9

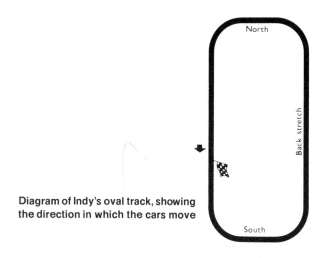

Diagram of Indy's oval track, showing the direction in which the cars move

Remembering what he had learned in Europe, Fisher finally came up with a solution to the two problems that concerned him. What America needed was a large, enclosed, oval-shaped course. Fisher imagined a race course where cars could be driven at high speeds for long periods of time, and where large numbers of spectators could be accommodated. This track would provide American car manufacturers with a proving ground, and it would also make American auto racing more popular. As racing expanded, the public would become more interested in buying passenger cars, and the automobile industry would be able to build *better* cars. It would be like one good neighbor helping another, knowing that sooner or later he would be helped in return.

After thinking and planning for several years, Fisher instructed a realtor to find a suitable piece of property. Meanwhile, he began looking for partners to join him in financing what would be a massive project. In December 1908, the group headed by Fisher paid $72,000 for 320 acres of land just northwest of Indianapolis, Indiana. A corporation valued at $250,000 was formed to construct the Indianapolis Motor Speedway by the following summer.

The investment was no small gamble. Fisher, the guiding force and inspiration behind the venture, knew that his idea would work. Yet, he must have had mixed feelings. As a practical businessman, he naturally expected to receive a reasonable profit someday. But his dream was to create an American

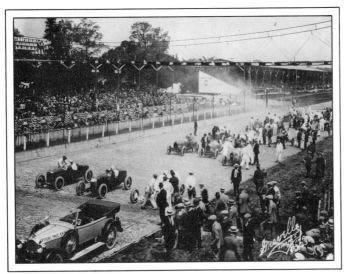
Starting lineup of the 1923 race

And after 1914, there were years when the owners of the Speedway put more money back into the property than they got out of it.

In 1927, Fisher and his associates sold the Speedway to Eddie Rickenbacker for $700,000. They could have gotten more money if they had sold it to real-estate developers. But the developers would have torn down the track to build other projects. Fisher insisted that the Speedway remain intact as the site of a great sports spectacle and testing ground. Rickenbacker agreed.

But 18 years later, Rickenbacker faced a problem. World War II had just ended. The track had been closed and neglected during four years of war. To restore the track would have been too expensive, so Rickenbacker decided to look for a buyer. He sought no profit from the sale—only a sum equal to what he had invested. Like Fisher, he could have done better by selling to people who

racing institution the worth of which could not be measured totally in dollars and cents. The leadership of Fisher—and later of Rickenbacker and of Hulman—was marked by dedication to the welfare of auto racing in general, and of the Speedway in particular. It wasn't until 1914 that the original owners received any profit from their investment.

wanted to use the Speedway for their own private gain. But he refused such offers.

In the end, the challenge of reviving the Indianapolis Motor Speedway fell to Tony Hulman, a well-known Indiana businessman and sportsman. Hulman appreciated the tradition connected with the Indianapolis 500. He wanted the race continued, desiring only enough income from each race to care for the property properly. It is anyone's guess as to whether or not Hulman has done as well as he thought he would since acquiring the Speedway in 1945. He keeps the earnings from admissions, concessions, and other sources a closely guarded secret. However, most of the profit is probably reinvested in the Speedway property.

Over the years, the value of the Indianapolis Motor Speedway has increased tremendously. If Hulman were to sell the 539-acre race course today, he could get close to $50 million for it. While he has no intention of selling now, there will, of course, be a new owner someday. Whoever the next owner is, he will have the responsibility for preserving an American tradition. It is almost unthinkable to racing fans that Speedway land would ever be used for anything other than what Carl Fisher envisioned for it many years ago.

Tony Hulman

# THE SPEEDWAY YESTERDAY

The history of the Indianapolis Motor Speedway has been far from smooth. Born after a long struggle, the Speedway grew up amid controversy and conflict to become the exciting racing center that it is today. Emotions run high at Indy because the stakes are so high. In such an atmosphere, people show both their best and their worst sides. Incidents and casual tales tend to become legends at Indy. From daily happenings at the track come memorable stories of triumph and defeat, joy and sorrow, humor and tragedy.

Some of the most dramatic stories about Indy come from the period of the track's earliest history. Carl Fisher, Indy's founder, soon discovered that getting financing for his idea had been easy compared to the problems that occurred in the spring and summer of 1909. Construction lagged behind schedule despite personal supervision by Fisher and frantic efforts by workmen. At the last minute, the entire length of the course had to be changed from three miles to two and a half miles in order to better fit the dimensions of the overall site. In addition to these problems, several tankloads of oil—which were to be used with crushed rock in the track's surface—were somehow lost enroute from Chicago, Illinois.

Work on the course was still in progress on June 5, 1909, when the Speedway hosted its opening event—a balloon race. About 3,500 people bought tickets, and about 40,000 watched free from outside the gates. The result was Indianapolis' first traffic jam, which ensnarled many paying customers and at least one guest of honor. The delayed guest was Indiana governor Thomas R. Marshall, who arrived about an hour after he was supposed to participate in opening ceremonies. Upon approaching the track area, the governor couldn't find a parking place. So he finally had to park in a farmer's barnyard and walk a mile to the track.

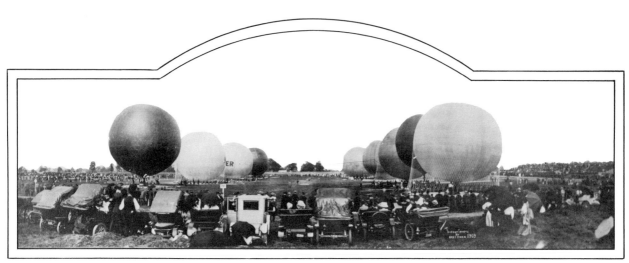

The Speedway's opening event in 1909—a balloon race

The Speedway's opening event was successful, but the track itself was still not ready for auto racing. For this reason, Fisher had to postpone some automobile races originally set for the July 4 weekend. By August, the track was nearing completion.

On August 15, 1909, motorcyclists arriving at the track for a series of national championship events were unhappy to see the crushed-rock surface. The cyclists claimed that the track was too dangerous to race on. After putting the track's safety to the test, they discovered that they were right. Most of the motorcycle races were eventually cancelled due to lack of entries.

On August 19, 1909, the Indianapolis Motor Speedway opened for three days of auto racing. But the races proved to be disastrous. The continual pounding of tires on the track sent pebbles flying in all directions. When ruts and chuckholes began to appear, accidents resulted. One accident claimed the lives of a driver, two mechanics, and two spectators.

It was a bitter, shocking experience for the Speedway owners. Their goal had been to construct a race track that would contribute to the development of better and safer automobiles. Yet the track that was supposed to make motoring safer was itself unsafe.

Fisher and his associates did not need the pressure they got from the drivers and the public to realize that something had to be done. Without hesitation they decided to repave the entire course with brick, the best and most expensive material available. The job took 63 days and required approximately 3,200,000 bricks. Since each brick weighed 10 pounds, an average workman handling from 200 to 250 bricks per hour lifted about 10 tons of bricks during his nine-hour shift.

Races resumed on the new track surface in December 1909. Races were also held over the Memorial Day, Fourth of July, and Labor Day holidays in 1910. Attendance was good. Publicity was favorable. Competition was exciting. And drivers and fans were pleased. Most important, there were no accidents.

But the owners were not content as they reviewed their progress and looked forward to the future. Fisher knew that the Speedway could become just another race course someday if steps were not taken to avoid it. Therefore, he suggested holding only *one* race per year, making that race longer than usual, and offering more prize money than any other speedway. This single event, he knew, would command the attention of the racing public and the automotive industry.

The start of a 1909 motorcycle race

Fisher's reasoning was accurate in every way. On Memorial Day, 1911, the first Indianapolis 500-mile race took place before a packed house of 80,000 thrilled spectators. Drivers battled for a $25,000 purse, an astonishing amount for that era. As Fisher anticipated, the 500-mile distance caught the imagination of the public. Until then, racing fans were used to viewing races of only 5 to 250 miles in length. But the new 500-mile distance was more in keeping with the purposes of Indy, for it vigorously tested both the cars and the drivers. Driver Ray Harroun won that first Indy 500 with an average speed

Race action from the first Indianapolis 500-mile race, 1911

of 74.59 miles per hour (mph). He was the first among scores of heroes at Indy, and the first about whom many stories have been told.

Fans identify with race-car drivers—they laugh with them, cry with them, and pray for them. This holds true for every driver, not just the winners. Not every Indy driver cheered by the crowd is a winner. Ralph DePalma, for example, was one of the most famous losers of all time. In the 1912 race, he held the lead until mechanical failure stopped him just a mile from the finish line. As Joe Dawson roared by him to victory, DePalma and his mechanic, Rupert Jeffkins, slowly climbed out of the car. DePalma said they might as well start pushing the car toward the pit area. The fans cheering Dawson gradually noticed DePalma and Jeffkins pushing their car. Immediately, sympathy for the driver who had come so close to winning swept over the stands. By the time the weary pair reached the finish line, the crowd's ovation was so deafening that winner Dawson was all but forgotten. Three years later, in 1915, DePalma finally won the Indy 500.

Ralph DePalma in his heyday

The respect and hero-worship that fans have for a race-car driver is justified. But in the history of the Indy 500, it has sometimes led to problems. Often in sports, the athletes or competitors have conflicts of interest with the owners or managers. Carl Fisher, Eddie Rickenbacker, and Tony Hulman all had to be determined enough to insist that the interests of the Speedway and the race were more

In early Indy races, mechanics rode with the drivers to keep them informed of the race action.

important than the interests of any individual or group.

One controversy caused by a conflict of interest was set off by driver Ralph DePalma. In 1916, DePalma demanded "appearance" money—money that would be given to him by the Speedway in return for his guarantee to enter the 500. Guarantees were permitted in other races for drivers as famous as De-Palma, but they were absolutely forbidden at Indy. A policy of guarantees at the Speedway could have led to its financial ruin. Therefore, despite DePalma's popularity, Fisher refused to give in to his demands. By the time DePalma finally dropped the issue and submitted his entry form, the deadline had already passed. So DePalma did not compete in the 1916 race.

Speedway rules were again challenged in 1933 when Rickenbacker was faced with a rebellion on the very morning of the race. One of the drivers, Howdy Wilcox, had qualified for a starting position several days earlier but then had failed to pass a medical examination. In support of Wilcox, the other drivers signed a statement refusing to drive unless Wilcox was allowed to participate. Rickenbacker was not swayed, however, and the rebellion fell apart.

In 1947, Hulman had to contend with a group of drivers who had formed their own professional association. This group went so far as to demand a guaranteed sum of money from the total amount taken in at the race.

The argument raged for several months before Hulman finally won out.

Many stories about Indy deal with conflict and controversy, but the Indianapolis Motor Speedway has had its lighter moments, too. One of these moments took place in 1913, when a Frenchman named Jules Goux won the Indy 500. During his pit stops, Goux repeatedly tried to communicate with his American chief mechanic, Johnny Aitkin. Finally, a translator told Aitkin that Goux wanted chilled wine to drink during his pit stops. This was out of the ordinary, to say the least, but Aitkin permitted one of the driver's friends to bring him six partially filled bottles of champagne. Five pit stops and five empty wine bottles later, Goux emerged the winner of the race. After the race, photographers snapped Goux waving an empty bottle and opening another. It was probably the only time that "hard spirits" replaced milk in the winner's traditional victory toast.

Another humorous incident at Indy in-

Jules Goux at the wheel, 1913. Riding as his observer was Georges Boillot.

volved driver Mario Andretti, who won the 1969 race. Andretti piloted a car owned by Andy Granatelli, a former driver who was now a sponsor. For 23 years, Granatelli had been trying to get into Victory Lane at Indy, as either a driver or a sponsor. When Andretti won, Granatelli was so happy that he grabbed Mario and kissed him even before the Indy 500 beauty queen had a chance to give Mario the traditional victory kiss!

Drivers are not the only people who play a part in the stories of the Indianapolis 500. A member of the press was involved in one of the most monumental mistakes in Indy history. In 1933 an editor of the Walsenburg, Colorado, *World-Independent* sent a telegram to the Associated Press news bureau asking for a story on the outcome of the race. The AP bureau chief replied, "Will Overhead Indianapolis Race Winner," which meant in newspaper terminology that he would send the results by regular Western Union telegram ("will overhead" = "will send by telegram"). The inexperienced editor, however, misunderstood AP's answer. On the afternoon of May 30, his newspaper reported, "Will Overhead Wins the Indianapolis Memorial Day Race." It was the first and last race ever "won" by that unknown driver, Will Overhead.

# THE SPEEDWAY TODAY

Age does not necessarily make a tradition out of an event. But a particular event cannot become a tradition unless it has survived over a long period of time.

The Indianapolis 500 is the oldest race of its kind in the United States, and its prestige has been maintained through the years. There has been a race every year since 1911, except in 1917 and 1918, during World War I, and between 1942 and 1945, during World War II.

The Indianapolis 500 succeeded because it was established at the right time, in the right place, and under the right leadership. When Indy came into being, road racing was well known in Europe but impractical in the United States. Thus, auto racing in this country had to develop purely American characteristics. The Indy 500 *was* a purely American concept in racing. It originated in the Midwest, where people were not too sophisticated for what amounted to a huge,

day-long picnic. And from the beginning, Speedway owners have been men devoted to racing; at no time have they been interested only in making the easy dollar.

Over the years, the Speedway has developed into the impressive racing facility that it is today. Wooden grandstands have been replaced by double-decked steel and concrete structures. There is reserved seating for about 230,000 spectators, almost three times the entire attendance at the first 500. Another 100,000 people can be accommodated in the infield, where there is also parking space for more than 25,000 cars. Four tunnels located at various points beneath the track provide access to the infield.

Some of the earlier landmarks of the Speedway are gone now, but they have not been forgotten. In 1913, a five-story structure was built on the inside edge of the race course overlooking the start-finish line. This structure served as an observation tower, a communication facility, and a press box. Called the Pagoda because of its Japanese-style architecture, it was a famous Speedway landmark for many years. Old-timers used to recall how the building swayed slightly from side to side as the occupants hustled from one window to another to watch the race.

In 1957, the timeworn Pagoda was swept aside in one phase of a $1-million improvement program instituted by Tony Hulman. On the former Pagoda site now stands a modern, seven-story tower with the finest possible viewing points for official timers, scorers, members of the press and radio commentators, the safety director, and other officials. The tower is flanked on either side by a 14,000-seat grandstand section called the Tower Terrace.

Also included in Hulman's 1957 improvement program was the remodeling of the pit area, the place where cars are serviced during a race. More working space was provided for the pit crews. A concrete retaining

The Pagoda, a Speedway landmark for 44 years

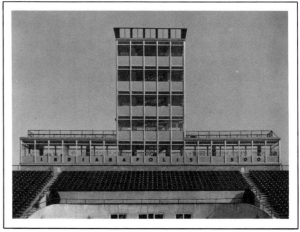

This modern tower replaced the Pagoda in 1957.

The Speedway's golf clubhouse and 18th green

Inside the Speedway Museum

wall and a 15-foot grass plot were installed to separate the pit area from the track. A 35-foot-wide driveway was also constructed to give drivers a safer route to and from the pits.

A new electric scoreboard that resembled a space needle was built in 1959. In 1961, the Paddock grandstand was constructed directly across the track from the Tower Terrace. Incorporated into the Paddock were additional facilities for the press and, at the top, special spectator boxes. Called the Paddock Penthouse, these special box seats are the most expensive at Indy, each one costing at least $40.

The 539 acres of Speedway property owned by Hulman also includes an 18-hole golf course outside the track boundary, a nine-hole golf course inside the track, a clubhouse, a 96-unit motel, and the Indianapolis Motor Speedway Museum. Built in 1956 and expanded several times since then, the museum is open to the public without charge. On display in the museum are etchings of each 500-mile race winner, as well as many interesting historical photos, trophies (some dating back to 1909), medals, racing programs, the first crash helmet worn in the United States, and other items of special interest. But the most impressive displays of all are the famous cars that have been driven at Indianapolis over the years. Visitors are not allowed to sit inside the cars or touch them, but they can look and let their imaginations take them back through the years.

Among the cars exhibited is the Marmon Wasp driven to victory by Ray Harroun in 1911, during the first Indy 500. So is the National that Joe Dawson drove past the frustrated Ralph DePalma in 1912. Another famous car on display at the Speedway museum is the Duesenberg that Jimmy Murphy drove to victory in the 1922 Indy 500. The year before, Murphy had become the first American race driver to win a European Grand Prix. He won it in the Duesenberg at LeMans, France. Yet another famous race car in the museum is the Italian Maserati that

Wilbur Shaw piloted to two of his three Indy victories (in 1939 and 1940). Later-model cars on display include those driven to victory by Mauri Rose in 1947 and 1948, Lee Wallard in 1951, Bill Vukovich in 1953 and 1954, Sam Hanks in 1957, and A. J. Foyt in 1964. Among the oldest cars in the museum are Carl Fisher's 1903 Premier and Louis Chevrolet's Buick, which won one of the races at the Speedway's inaugural program in 1909.

Carl Fisher's 1903 Premier

The music of marching bands fills the air as fans make their way to their seats. In the pits, the cars are ready to go.

25

Against a backdrop of gasoline fumes, a car is wheeled onto the track.

Driver Mario Andretti races close to the wall during the 1973 Indy 500.

At race's end, the winner is given a rousing reception in Victory Lane.
Here, Al Unser celebrates his second consecutive Indy victory, 1971.

The heart of the Speedway is, of course, the track itself. The track is two and a half miles long, and fans can ride its entire length in a special sightseeing bus. The track's asphalt surface was installed by Eddie Rickenbacker, who paved all but the main straightaway in 1935. In 1961 the straightaway was paved with asphalt, except for a 36-inch strip of original brick at the starting line. The brick was left for sentimental reasons. The Speedway's nickname, "The Brickyard," came into being in 1909, when bricks were used to replace the crushed-rock surface.

The dimensions of the track are the same today as they were in 1909. The width varies from 50 feet on the straightaways to 60 feet on the turns. Each of the four turns measures one-quarter mile in length and is banked at an angle of 12 degrees and 9 minutes. The short straightaways at the north and south ends measure one-eighth of a mile, and the front and back straightaways measure five-eighths of a mile each.

On a track of these dimensions there is a limit to "safe" racing speeds. If you ask an Indy driver what that limit is, he will probably say he doesn't know. He only knows that he will push his car as fast as he possibly can—just as those who came before him and those who will come after him. At the same time, however, race participants as well as spectators must be protected from personal injury. In assuming this responsibility, Speedway and USAC officials must choose between keeping the course as up to date as the cars or reducing the speed of the cars. The protection of human life must remain the Speedway's first responsibility.

# MAY AT INDY

Officially, the Indianapolis 500-mile race begins at 10 A.M. on one of the days during the Memorial Day weekend. Unofficially, it begins about 30 days earlier with the arrival of racing teams—cars, owners, drivers, chief mechanics, crews—at "Gasoline Alley," the garage area behind the Tower Terrace.

The term *Gasoline Alley* has no great significance in today's vocabulary. But in the early 1900s, there must have been scores of "gasoline alleys" leading to sheds or stables where young men tinkered with the amazing new automobile. A cartoonist named Frank King gave the term national recognition when, in 1919, he introduced the comic strip "Gasoline Alley." This cartoon is still carried by many newspapers.

Many Indy 500 races are won or lost days and weeks before the race, and it's what happens in Gasoline Alley that makes all the difference. Driving skill, as the drivers themselves know, is only one of the important factors in determining a winner. Other factors include the quality of the car, the work of mechanics and pit crews, and just plain luck. Of course there is nothing anyone can do about luck. Most race-car drivers believe that "what will happen, will happen." But of all the factors that could possibly influence the outcome of a race, perhaps the mechanics in Gasoline Alley are the most important. Mechanics work many hours—most of the night as race day nears—adjusting and re-adjusting automobile parts in order to produce maximum speed and handling efficiency in the machine.

While it's every man for himself on race day, a "buddy" feeling exists among the crews during the month of May. Lending and borrowing of tools is as normal as asking a friend for the time of day. This same feeling of mutual cooperation was apparent early in

the morning of the 1941 race, when a trickle of gasoline was suddenly ignited by sparks from a welder's torch. In minutes, the garages were ablaze, and the fire was spreading rapidly from one garage to another. Firemen rushed to the emergency, but had it not been for the quick action of racing crews on the scene, many race cars would have been destroyed. After pushing their own cars to safety, the crews battered open the locked doors of other garages and saved their rivals' racers. Only three cars were lost, despite the fact that half of Gasoline Alley had been leveled by the fire. Later that morning, teams

Against a background of smoldering ruins, observers survey the charred wreck of a $50,000 race car destroyed in the 1941 Gasoline Alley fire.

whose garages were still standing shared their space and tools with those less fortunate. Preparations for the race continued, and the race took place as planned.

An automobile race the size of the Indy 500 requires a great deal of organization. All activity on the track—practice runs, time trials, the race itself—is supervised by the United States Auto Club. Supervision of the racing activities begins even before the practice runs are made. First, a driver and his car must pass inspection before they are allowed on the track. Every driver must pass a physical examination, and every car must measure up to certain specifications. Practically every part of the racing machine is governed in some manner by competition rules. In all, there are 20 different measurements that must be scientifically tested for endurance. Even after a car passes inspection, it is continually under observation in the pits and on the track.

Rookies—drivers new to Indy—must first demonstrate their skills at controlled speeds before being permitted to qualify for the race. This has been a Speedway requirement since 1936. It was established because first-year pilots were involved in more accidents than veteran drivers. A driver may be a champion in other racing fields and may have as many as 10 years of racing experience behind him. Yet, if he's new to Indy, he's still considered a "rookie," and he must prove that he belongs on the track.

Each year, hopeful owners bring a total of 80 to 90 cars to Indianapolis. Only 33 of these cars will qualify. To qualify, the cars compete against the clock in time trials held on the two weekends preceding the race. For some participants, these trials are as nerve-racking and exciting as the actual race. A few tenths of a second lost on a turn, for instance, can mean the difference between starting in the front row, the fifth or sixth row, or possibly not qualifying at all.

The time trials consist of four laps—10 miles—around the course. Each driver is allowed three "warm-up" laps before beginning his qualification run. If the driver and his team are not satisfied with the performance on the warm-up laps, they do not have to make the qualification run at that time. However, the driver will be put at the end of the line, and he must wait for an opportunity to qualify later. Even during the qualification run, the crew chief—who is carefully timing the car—can declare the run "abandoned" for any reason and call the car in. For the most part, time trials are a guessing game. Racing teams must estimate whether their car is traveling fast enough or whether it should be taken back to Gasoline Alley for adjustments. They must also weigh the effects of track conditions and weather conditions on present and future qualifying attempts.

After 33 cars have officially posted times,

the "bumping" begins. There are 50 or more drivers still waiting for their chance to achieve a better time than the earlier qualifiers. As one car earns a spot in the 11-row lineup (three cars to a row), all of the slower cars are forced back one place, and the slowest is bumped from the lineup completely. Drivers who have been bumped may try to regain a place in the field, driving a different car. One year, Jim MacElreath qualified, was bumped, qualified in a second car, was bumped, and qualified for a third time in a third car, only to be bumped once more.

Luck sometimes plays as big a part in time trials as it does in the actual race. During his 1950 qualifying run, Walt Faulkner electrified the crowd by appearing to increase speed on the turns instead of slowing down as usual. By the end of his run, which qualified him for the pole position, he was drenched in sweat. The reason he had gone so fast, according to one story, was that his throttle had been stuck since the first lap!

Qualifications end at 6 P.M. on the Sunday before the race. Inevitably there are cars still lined up waiting for one more chance — a chance that will not come, at least not that year. For some, the disappointment is almost unbearable. For those who made it, there is grateful celebration.

Other preparations for the race are being made during May too. The Speedway, which maintains a permanent year-round staff of about 100 people, hires thousands more for race day. The safety patrol alone totals approximately 2,400. Seven first-aid tents are set up, with a staff of more than 100 trained people. Twelve ambulances are readied. In the main Speedway hospital and in the stands, more than 250 doctors and nurses are on duty. Other people working with the Speedway staff include 135 men and women from the telephone company, 50 Western Union operators, 350 representatives from the United States Auto Club, 250 firemen, and 350 city, county, and state police.

The "500 Festival" organization, formed in 1957, sponsors various promotional activities, including a golf tournament, a queen's ball, a mayor's breakfast, and a gigantic downtown parade with floats, marching bands, and scores of celebrities. Among the well-known individuals who have participated in recent years are Jimmy Stewart, Lorne Green, Jim Garner, Kent McCord and Martin Milner of the "Adam 12" TV show, Joe Garagiola, Buddy Ebsen, Walter Cronkite, and astronauts Gordon Cooper, Pete Conrad, and the late Gus Grissom.

On the night before the race, fans begin gathering at the Speedway's 21 entrances. At 4 A.M. the gates open, and people and vehicles pour in as though they were on a treasure hunt. Soon the infield is a sea of cars, trucks, campers, limousines, and tents. Lanterns dot the area. Music and cooking begin. The grandstands fill up. It's one vast, carnival-like family picnic.

In Gasoline Alley, the cars and drivers are as ready as they will ever be. By 7:30 A.M. the sleek, colorful machines stand ready in their respective pit areas. About an hour later, the bands begin playing and marching. And at 9 A.M. the cars are wheeled into their starting positions on the track. Celebrities are presented to the huge throng. The "Star Spangled Banner" is played. Then there's a solemn hush, and all heads bow for the Memorial Day bugle taps honoring the war dead and the drivers who have lost their lives at Indy. At approximately 9:50 A.M. a guest vocalist sings the traditional "Back Home in Indiana." Somewhere on the grounds a tent is opened and thousands of colorful, helium-filled balloons float into the air.

Finally the moment is at hand for Tony Hulman to say the words that send chills up and down the spines of racing fans: "Gentlemen, start your engines!" Before the last echo of his voice dies out, it is lost in the roar of 33 engines revving up in ear-shattering readiness.

The greatest race course in the world is about to have its day once again.

Getting ready to race

# THE RACE

Bill Vukovich, two-time winner of the Indy 500, believed in giving a simple answer to questions about driving at the Speedway. "All you do," he said, "is step on the throttle and keep turning left."

There are 200 laps and 800 left-hand turns required to complete 500 miles at Indy. Charging with cold fury, Vukovich took those turns faster than anybody else in his day. Despite his simple description of the race, he knew what a complicated challenge it is to compete at Indy. For one thing, that smooth asphalt surface is, after all, not *perfectly* smooth. There is a tiny bump here, a slight variation in the banking there. These slight variations are magnified a hundred times over when you're coming off a straightaway at 200 miles per hour. Besides variations in road surface, wind is also a constant risk. It is possible that a sudden gust of wind, occurring at a certain moment, could transform a racer into an airborne missile. Perhaps this explains what happened to driver Jim Malloy, who was killed on a practice run in 1972. Heading into the third turn, Malloy's car abruptly turned sideways and nose-dived into the wall.

In addition to factors like wind and road surface, imagine the problems of driving in close formation, wheel to wheel and nose to tail. While traveling closely together at high speeds, the drivers must fight for their own "grooves," the pathways on the track that allow maximum speed for their particular car. At full throttle, the cars run as close as six feet from the outer concrete retaining wall on the straightaway. They dive so low going into the turns that they nearly go off the inside apron. And then coming off the turns, they drift outward toward the wall again until they almost scrape it. It is obvious that an error in judgment could result in immediate contact with either the wall or another car.

Some of the most dangerous moments at Indy occur at the very start of the race. The cars—33 of the fastest machines in the world—follow the pace car around the track for at least one full lap. Then the pace car increases its speed to over 100 mph in order to provide a "flying start" for the racers behind it. When the individual rows of cars are evenly lined up, the pace car darts off the track, the green "go" sign is flashed, and every car bursts forward with the acceleration of 700 or more horsepower.

In 1958, Dick Rathmann and Ed Elisian battled ferociously for the lead. On the third turn they sideswiped each other, causing a series of collisions that killed driver Pat O'Connor and wrecked eight cars. In 1964, a fiery crash on the second lap took the lives of rookie Dave MacDonald and popular veteran Eddie Sachs. The track was so littered with debris from their cars and five others that the race, for the first time in history, had to be stopped and restarted later.

The pace car darts into the pits, the green light flashes, and the race is on.

Normally, after an accident, the remaining cars continue running under a yellow light that means "drive with caution and maintain position."

After the 1964 tragedy, the United States Auto Club required that fuel tanks be constructed of metal, with rubber liners. These tanks, USAC ruled, could not extend beyond

Salt Walther's car burns after crashing in the first lap of the 1973 Indy 500.

the inside edge of the wheels and could not be placed directly in front of the driver. Sachs' car had had an extra gasoline tank in the nose, and it had exploded upon impact with MacDonald's wreckage.

The new ruling possibly saved some lives in 1966 when, for the second time in Indy history, the race had to be stopped. Even before reaching the first turn, 16 cars were involved in a chaotic chain of smashups. Eleven of the cars were too badly damaged to continue. Of these, only one car caught fire, but miraculously no one was injured.

In 1973 another terrible accident occurred in the mad scramble after the green flag. David ("Salt") Walther's racer veered into a fence, burst into flames, and bounded down the track, causing other collisions. Walther was critically burned, three other drivers suffered minor injuries, and about a dozen spectators were hit by flying debris. The race was halted and then postponed because of rain. Rain continued the next day, causing yet another postponement of the race. The third day finally saw the running of the official 1973 Indianapolis 500, but another downpour resulted in the completion of only 133 of the 200 scheduled laps. During those laps, the most tragic incidents of the 1973 race occurred. Driver Swede Savage lost control of his car on the 58th lap, crashed, and later died of his injuries. In a second accident, a rescue truck speeding to help Savage struck and killed Armondo Teran, a mechanic.

To Indy officials, incidents like these point to the urgent need for improved safety regulations at the Speedway. The officials also feel, however, that serious crashes are the exception rather than the rule, and they emphasize that most of the races are decided on the merit of cars, drivers, and crews.

The challenge of the Indy 500 by necessity creates personal resources in the drivers who compete there. Strategy, for example, has been important from the very first Indy 500. In that first race, Ray Harroun drove a car with a single-seat cockpit instead of one with a second seat for a mechanic. Some people objected to this for reasons of safety because, in those days, a mechanic rode with the driver as his observer. Harroun feared that he might be ruled out of the race for excluding his observer, so he installed a mirror through which he could see the drivers behind him. Harroun thus made popular what would soon become a standard automobile part—the rearview mirror.

Patience is a necessity and often a winning virtue at Indy. For example, Harroun did not have the fastest car in the 1911 race, but he drove the best race. In order to get maximum mileage out of his tires, he set a steady pace for himself. Even when others whizzed by him, he patiently plodded along at his own pace. It happened that Harroun simply outlasted the more powerful cars—they had to make more stops for tire changes than he did.

There are other examples of patience winning over speed. Louis Meyer, a three-time Indy winner, started in the 28th position in 1936 and kept moving up as car after car dropped out with mechanical failure. In 1957,

Ray Harroun won the 1911 race with the help of his own invention—a rear-view mirror.

Sam Hanks studied leader Paul Russo's technique of accelerating out of the turns. Hanks studied this technique for 20 laps before deciding how, when, and where he would overtake Russo for the win. A. J. Foyt won the 1967 race when the revolutionary turbocar driven by Parnelli Jones failed on the 197th lap, giving Foyt the lead.

Persistence is another necessary characteristic of Indy hopefuls, most of whom,

**Wilbur Shaw won in 1937, setting a record speed of 113 mph.**

out how much slower he could afford to go without being overtaken by the second-place man, Ralph Hepburn. It happened that Shaw won by 2.16 seconds, the closest finish in Indy history. In later years Shaw won two more 500s. In 1945, when Tony Hulman bought the Speedway, Shaw was appointed president and general manager. He held this position until his death in a plane crash in 1954.

unfortunately, never see their hopes come true. Racing greats such as Tony Bettenhausen, Rex Mays, Ted Horn, and many others have never won the Indianapolis 500. Wilbur Shaw tried for 10 frustrating years before finally winning in 1937. After leading for most of that race, Shaw saw his oil pressure gauge begin to drop. Quickly, he figured

During a race, the amount of time a driver spends in his pit stops is important in determining his finish. In 1929, Louis Meyer lost the race because he killed his engine during his last pit stop. It took seven minutes to get the car started again, and the delay cost him the victory. Winner Ray Keech finished ahead of Meyer by 6 minutes and 14 seconds.

Another example is the very close 1961 race between Eddie Sachs and A. J. Foyt. Foyt was leading the race until he made an unexpected pit stop on his 184th lap. He needed fuel because of a refueling failure on the previous stop. Sachs took the lead, but then *he* had to make an unscheduled stop for a tire change on the 198th lap. By that time Foyt was back on the track and making up for lost time. Foyt won the race over Sachs by a mere 8.2 seconds.

The importance of pit work was evident in 1962, when Roger Ward, Len Sutton, and Eddie Sachs finished one-two-three within 31 seconds of each other. Sachs' pit stops took 20 seconds longer than Sutton's, which was exactly the number of seconds that Sachs finished behind Sutton.

Because precious race time can be lost in the pits, crew chiefs practice pit-stop assignments constantly. Crews must be able to refuel a car and make tire changes in less than half a minute. Often, crews can do these things in only 20 seconds. Even faster pit stops are possible now that tires normally last the full 500 miles. But crews have to be ready for any emergency.

Unexpected problems sometimes develop during a race, so it is important that a driver and his pit crew communicate well. A pit crew sends messages to its driver on a "pit board," a small blackboard held at trackside so the driver can see the message as he whizzes by. If a driver has to alert his crew, he uses hand signals. The crew can then prepare for an upcoming emergency pit stop.

One of the most memorable pit stops in recent years involved Lloyd Ruby in 1969. Due to lack of proper communication with his crew, Ruby started to leave the pit before one of the refueling hoses had been removed from his car. As a result, the fuel tank in Ruby's car was almost destroyed, and he was out of the race.

A good car. Skill. A good crew. Luck. You have to have it all to win at Indy.

# AFTER THE RACE

Mark Donohue in Victory Lane, 1972

No one likes to lose. Losing is especially hard for a very competitive person. But it is often easier for a person to accept a loss by a wide margin than a loss by a slim one. For example, baseball teams would rather be trounced 18 to 2 than be defeated by one run in an extra inning. A politician who loses by a fraction of a percentage point does a lot more soul-searching the next day than one who is buried by a landslide of votes.

Many of the losers each year at Indy are not surprised or disappointed, for they did not really expect to win. Cars starting in the ninth, tenth, or eleventh rows are simply not fast enough, ordinarily, to catch the racers that qualified far ahead of them. If the end cars *do* catch up, it is because of an unusual number of mechanical failures and accidents ahead of them. But the closer a driver actually comes to being a contender, the more it hurts to see somebody else wheel his car into Victory Lane.

Parnelli Jones on his way to victory in the controversial 1963 race

The pressure of competing at Indy is so intense that it sometimes bubbles over at race's end, like boiling water. After the 1963 race, some drivers thought winner Parnelli Jones' car had been spilling oil on the track, causing their machines to slide out of control. Jones answered hotly that the oil had come from other racers. At a noon luncheon the next day, the smoldering controversy exploded again, leading to an actual punching and wrestling match between Jones and Eddie Sachs.

In 1947, driver Bill Holland was extremely bitter about his loss to Mauri Rose. Both men were driving cars owned by Lou Moore. Toward the end of the race, Holland and Rose seemed to have the first-place and second-place spots clinched. Moore did not want them to engage in a duel that could knock both of them out of position, so he flashed the "take it easy" sign. Holland, running in first place, slowed up and was overtaken by Rose, who had continued at his same speed. Holland, thinking he had a full lap lead, smiled and waved Rose by him. The next lap around, Moore gave both of them the "OK" sign, the signal that they were in the clear for the final lap. At race's end, Holland thought he had been tricked when he discovered that he had lost the race. He had not had a full lap lead after all. But most racing experts felt that it was Holland's own responsibility to have known what lap he and his closest rival were on.

Mistakes in judgment, freak accidents, mechanical problems—all of these things naturally frustrate and anger hopeful drivers. Bill Vukovich, for example, was furious after the 1952 race. The steering assembly on his car broke when he had only 10 laps to go. Troy Ruttman won, and Vukovich dropped from the lead to a 17th-place finish.

Vukovich's bad luck calls to mind an incident that occurred 32 years earlier to the Chevrolet brothers—Art, Louis, and Gaston. Eager to win, the brothers had entered seven cars in the race. But, one by one, their cars dropped out because of faulty steering arms. Only the car driven by Gaston Chevrolet held together long enough to win. Afterward, Louis Chevrolet, still mad about the fate of his family's other entries, angrily kicked the steering arm of Gaston's car. That arm promptly fell off, too.

Drivers enter their first turn following the start of the 1952 Indy 500.

Drivers are aware, of course, of the possible consequences if machinery should break on them in the fury of a race. They are not fools. But they are not afraid, either. They accept the risks as part of their business, or they don't race. "When it's not fun anymore," said two-time winner Roger Ward after

Troy Ruttman, winner of the 1952 race, tries to beat out a gasoline fire during his pit stop.

failing to finish in 1966, "that's the time to get out." So he did.

From the standpoint of timing, Sam Hanks was more fortunate. He went out a winner. After winning the 1957 Indy 500, Hanks announced his retirement at the celebration in Victory Lane. He was the first driver to retire in this way since Ray Harroun in 1911.

A driver who reaches Indy's Victory Lane is on top of the auto-racing world. After his victory, his car is displayed on the black-and-white checkered carpet in front of the main grandstand. He drinks from the traditional bottle of milk. The symbolic wreath of triumph is placed around his neck. He is interviewed over the Speedway's public address system and also over the Speedway's nationwide radio network of 700 stations. If the victor never wins another race, he has had his moment of glory, his piece of racing immortality.

For all the participants, the pot at the end of the rainbow becomes even richer the next night at the victory dinner. More than $1 million in prize money is distributed among all the drivers. Over one-quarter of that amount is shared by the winning driver, the car owner, and the crew. Money is also awarded for leading a lap, and drivers who have led a good many laps earn a large sum.

The checkered flag waves a winner home.

All 33 participants are well rewarded financially for just qualifying in the race.

Most of the prize money comes from the Speedway organization, but not all of it. The Indianapolis Chamber of Commerce, through a special fund-raising committee, has provided donations since 1920. In addition, approximately 60 individuals and companies offer cash or merchandise awards and trophies. Usually, these givers seek the publicity that comes with making a large donation to the Speedway. But, in the words of Tony Hulman, the donors also give out of a "love of motor racing and an interest in the development of the motor car. . . ."

Whatever his reason for giving or whatever his fate on the track, each donor and each hopeful driver helps to form the backbone of this great American racing tradition, the Indy 500.

# LAST IMPRESSIONS

If Carl Fisher were alive today, he would not be at all surprised by the prestige of the Indianapolis 500-mile race. But he *would* be surprised by the changes in the Speedway and in the cars that compete there. The "Indy racer" of today is a special type of racing car that travels the United States Auto Club's championship-car circuit. These Indy cars are as different from those of Fisher's day as modern passenger cars are from the first horseless carriages.

Today's Indy racers are light, weighing about 1,350 pounds without driver or fuel. They are low-slung; that is, they ride low to the ground. The driver sits in a seat that is specially made for him. He rides so low in the car that his line of vision is only about 16 inches off the ground. The car is powered by a rear engine whose turbocharger adds horsepower by providing a better fuel and air mixture. The car's rear tires grip the road surface with treads up to 16 inches wide. Certain design improvements, such as "wings," enable the car to hug the track better at high speeds.

The racer does not look like the ordinary passenger car. But automotive engineers have used the racer in order to develop and improve the passenger car, just as Fisher intended. When an Indy car travels 150 mph or more for 500 miles, the engineer gets as much data on the car's endurance as he would from studying 50,000 or even 100,000 miles of travel on a passenger car. Racers must do everything passenger cars do—accelerate, turn, brake—but they must do these things better. Under the punishing conditions of high-speed racing, flaws are exposed much sooner than they would be otherwise.

High-compression engines. Torsion bars. Four-wheel brakes. Better fuels and lubricants. Hydraulic shock absorbers. Better chassis designs. Lighter, more durable metal construction. Fuel injector systems. Improved spark plugs and piston rings. Safer, longer-lasting, more skid-free tires. All of these features were developed at the Speedway and were gradually included in passenger cars.

But the cost has been high. In only an instant, a $100,000 racer can be "totaled out," completely wrecked. Owners of race cars are not usually in the racing business for money. If they win just enough races to pay for car repairs or for building or buying new racers, they generally consider themselves lucky. Dollar costs can be measured, but loss of lives cannot. Bill Vukovich, Tony Bettenhausen, Eddie Sachs and many others won fame and fortune at Indy. They also died there.

Driver Barney Oldfield and Henry Ford with the Ford 999, an early race car

Johnny Rutherford, winner of the 1974 Indy 500, in a modern racer

Has Indy been worth the price? There is no direct answer. No one forces a businessman to invest his last nickel in sponsoring a car at Indy. And no one forces a driver to put on his fire-resistant underwear, fire-resistant uniform, flameproof gloves, crash helmet, face mask, and ear plugs to climb into a car that could become his coffin. He races because something inside him *needs* the challenge of high-speed competition. If no progress had been made in American auto racing since early in the century, and if racing were still done on small dirt tracks, that is where you would find the Vukoviches, Sachses, and Bettenhausens.

Indy drivers risk their lives for a trophy, money, a speed record, or the thrill of pitting their skills against those of other drivers. Meanwhile, we learn from them, are excited by their courage, identify with their efforts, and benefit from their pioneering. This is what makes the Indianapolis 500 a tradition that grows stronger every time the song "Back Home in Indiana" is followed by the stirring command "Gentlemen, start your engines!"

## THE RACING BOOKS

*DRAG RACING*
*ICE RACING*
*MOTORCYCLE RACING*
*ROAD RACING*
*SNOWMOBILE RACING*
*TRACK RACING*
*AMERICAN RACE CAR DRIVERS*
*INTERNATIONAL RACE CAR DRIVERS*
*THE INDIANAPOLIS 500*

*We specialize in publishing quality books for
young people. For a complete list please write:*

Lerner Publications Company
241 First Avenue North, Minneapolis, Minnesota 55401